MEXICO

Texts by

Edgar Bustamente / Jesús Romé

Crescent Books

Distributed by Crown Publishers, Inc.

Text pages 3 to 29 Edgar Bustamente;
pages 29 to 95: Jesús Romé.

*Credits: A & B/Ricciarini: 64a - 69b - 84b - 109a, b, d -
111 - Bevilacqua/Ricciarini: 95b - Carmi/Neri: 5 - 6b - 46a -
70a - 78a, b, c - 106 - Carot/Fotogram: 64a - 66 - Ciriani/
Ricciarini: 16 - 44 - 62 - 80 - 81 - 82 - 84a - 100b - 105a - Conti:
3 - 6a - 7 - 11a - 14b - 15b - 18 - 25 - 28c - 30 - 31 - 36 - 41a -
48a, b, c - 51 - 52a - 53a - 54a, b - 55 - 56a, b - 58a - 71 - 89a, b -
90a, b, c - 94a, b - 95a - 96b - 97a, b, c - 98a, b - 99a, b, c, d -
102a, b - 103a - 108a, b - Fiore: End papers - 8a, b, c - 9a, b -
13a, b - 14a - 15a - 27a - 28b - 37a, b - 38 - 39a, b - 45a - 50 -
52b - 53b - 59 - 74a, b - 75c, d - 76a, b, c - 91 - 93a - 96a - 100a -
101a, b - 104 - 107 - 112 - Gaugez/Fotogram: 69a - Gerster:
11b - 33 - 46b - 47 - 47b - 58b - 61 - 63a, b - 65b - 68 - 72 - 86 -
110b - Giraudon: 34 - Henneghien/Fotogram: 77 - 110a -
Marcardi/Neri: 40 - Masson/Fotogram: 105b - Pillonnel/
Fotogram: 19 - Seemuller: 21 - 22 - 23 - 28a - 41b - 42 - 43 -
45b - 64b - 65a - 70b - 74b - 79 - 85 - 87 - Unedi: 27b - 39c - 60 -
73 - 75a - 92 - 93b - 103b - 109b - Vignes: 18b - 29 - 32 - Viol-
let: 49.*

First English edition published by
Editions Minerva S.A., Genève.

Library of Congress Catalog
Card Number: F1216.B8413 972 79-9955

I.S.B.N. 0-517-282828

This edition is distributed by Crescent Books,
a division of Crown Publishers, Inc.

a b c d e f g h

© *Editions Minerva S.A., Genève, 1977*

Printed in Italy

In order to understand Mexico and get to know it more thoroughly than a tourist on a brief visit, it is essential to remember the sheer strength of the contradictions between the Indian and the Spanish elements in its past. The mixture of these two peoples, the merging of two races and two cultures, one of them for many years subordinate to the other, did not take place without difficulties. Teotihuacan, Tula, Palenque or Chichen-Itza bear a living witness to the harmony of one of those civilisations, while the splendid unity of the Plaza del Zócalo, the churches, convents, Baroque chapels which one comes across even in the most remote and humble places, show us the elegance of the other.

The great period of the history of Mexico spanning the 15 or 20,000 years between the first Asiatic migrations across the Bering land bridge and the year 1519, when the Aztecs thought that Hernán Cortés was the image of their own god, Quetzalcoatl, has absolutely no point of contact with Castille. Yet, once the troops of that Spanish kingdom had set foot on the soil of Mexico, the country's history was, forever after, to be influenced by Spanish attitudes and culture.

In order to form an idea of Tenochtitlan, on the ruins of which the capital of modern Mexico was built, we can study the reproduction of the ancient Aztec city in the National Museum of

Facing, the famous Plaza de las Tres Culturas, in Mexico City. Below: popular suburban market. Right: this young boy is already in business!

Anthropology, or the fresco by Diego Rivera depicting the market of that period. These pictures help explain the astonishment of the *conquistadores* when they first reached these cities. Even today, Tenochtitlan, which was built in the midst of a lake, is still the pride of Mexico. The charm of the capital lies precisely in the confrontation of the "Three Cultures" (Aztec, colonial and contemporary) which co-exist on the land which covers what was once a lake.

Besides the duality of its indigenous and Spanish elements, Mexico is a land of great contrasts between city and country, steep valleys and volcanic peaks, arid regions, tropical forests, the exuberant vegetation of Palenque and the numerous species of cactus to be found in the northern deserts.

While the larger cities have a modern, even futuristic appearance, rather like Mexico City itself, the country villages continue to cling to their traditions. Life in them proceeds at a leisurely pace, and the traveller who is looking for a real change from his daily routine back home will be fully satisfied. As long as he shows a certain minimum of discretion and is prepared, from time to time, to put away his camera, he will meet with a warm welcome everywhere he goes, and will not be regarded as an intruder. He will be able to relax and enjoy the kindness and the lively imagination of the Mexicans.

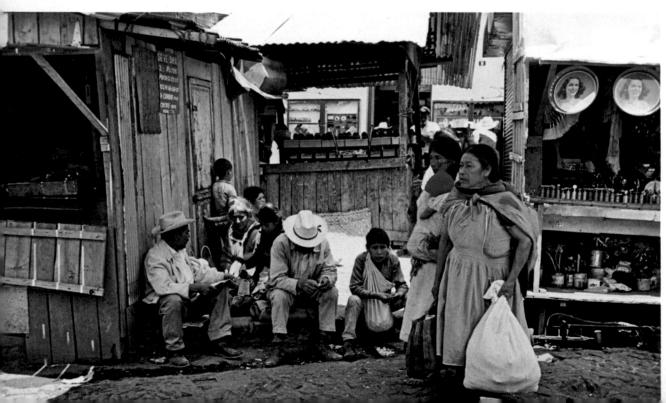

The Mexican sense of national identity is eloquently defined in an inscription carved on a plain stone wall in the Plaza de las Tres Culturas, in Mexico City, which reads: "On August 13 1521, Tlatelolco fell into the hands of Hernan Cortés, despite heroic resistance by Cuauthemoc. It was neither a triumph nor a defeat: it was the painful birth of the people of mixed blood which is the Mexico of today."

This mixed nature is also reflected in the different buildings to be found on the same square: the ruins of a pre-Hispanic temple erected by the Tlatelolcs, the Franciscan church and the adjacent college of Santa Cruz de Tlatelolco, now reconstructed, and an impressive set of tall apartment buildings, with more than 70,000 inhabitants.

In 1337 a group of Aztec dissidents who had founded Tenochtitlan in 1325 settled in Tlatelolco. The Tlatelolcs built their temple in 1378 and remained independent until a disastrous war with the Mexicas, which led to the overthrow of their monarch Moquihuix in 1473, and the subjugation of an entire people. Thenceforth the Tlatelolcs were governed by Aztec military rulers.

In its heyday, Tlatelolco was the site of a very advanced and prosperous market. In his *True History of the New Spain* Bernal Diaz del Castillo, a celebrated historian of this part of the Spanish Empire, gave a detailed description of the extraordinary atmosphere at this market, and the flourishing business which was done there. According to the croniclers, more than 60,000 people passed through its gates every day The Anthropological Museum in Mexico City contains a huge and strikingly lifelike model of a typical everyday scene in the market.

The name of Tlatelolco is also associated with the heroism and martyrdom of a people. As ruler of Tlatelolco and Emperor of the Aztecs, Cuauthemoc was the last leader of the indigenous resistance to the conquering Spanish forces under Hernán Cortés. When his uncle, Emperor Moctezuma II, died, he was only 26. Cuitlahuac, the emperor's successor, also died, from smallpox—incidentally, one of the white invaders' best allies during the conquest—only four months after coming to power. Cuauthemoc was therfore elected king while in the flower of his youth. At once, he set about dispelling the "phantom of uncertainty" which had plagued Moctezuma, and firmly resolved to fight, if need be, to the last man. Thus committed, and despite signs of mounting adversity, this brave man, like the perfect classical hero, led his people in a fight against inevitable doom.

At Tlatelolco, Cuauthemoc, the personification of his people's impending despair, fought one last action against Cortés who had

5

Various views of Mexico City: above, some modern office buildings. Below: fountain in Alameda Park. Facing: the famous Latin America Tower building. Right-hand page: the glorieta of Columbus and the Avenida F. Madero.

at his disposal an army which consisted of 86 horses, 194 crossbows and muskets, 700 infantrymen with swords and shields, 3 big cannon and 10 bushels of gunpowder. In addition, Cortés had the support of another 50,000 men from the allied tribes.

The tragic struggle of the last Aztec emperor has been eloquently described by Octavio Paz, the great Mexican poet and writer, as follows: "Cuauthemoc knew that he was doomed: his tragedy lies precisely in this inner acceptance of defeat. The entire history of Mexico seems to be permeated by the sense of total collapse which he must have felt as he saw the gods who had made his people great reduced to rubble. Cuauthemoc and his people died alone, forsaken by friends, allies, vassals and gods: like orphans they were left entirely to their own resources."

The siege of Tlatelolco lasted 75 days, during which the stench of death spread along streets and canals, against a background of horrendous war-cries or the piercing shrieks of the defenders. As the days went by, Cortés sought to save his men and what remained of the city by calling on Cuauthemoc to surrender. Negotiations began, but the Aztec emperor took advantage of the truce in order to restore his defenses and assemble his warriors. Though the corpses lay piled up in the streets, Cuauthemoc fought on, against all the odds. His sole desire was to kill as many Spanish troops as possible before the final collapse. Eventually, however, the end came in quite a different way. As Cuauthemoc was trying to rally his tattered army, he was taken prisoner and led before Cortés. According to Bernal Díaz del Castillo, he addressed his conqueror in these words: "I have done my duty in the defense of my people and my city. I can do no more. I have come before you as a prisoner. Take your dagger from your belt and kill me." This happened on August 13 1521, the day in the church calendar on which the martyr St. Hippolytus was honored; a violent thunderstorm lasted until midnight. Cortés was at last the undisputed master of Mexico. The death, on that same day, of a religion, a culture, a mode of government and a race, was to herald the birth, in tragic circumstances, of the rootless country of mixed blood that is Mexico today.

By a quirk of history, almost four and a half centuries after the fall of Tlatelolco, another disaster occurred on precisely the same spot, now known as the Plaza de las Tres Culturas. The date was October 2 1968, when Mexico City was preparing to hold the Olympic Games. The games coincided with a period of deep social unrest in Mexico; reform-minded groups, particularly those at the University of Mexico, were in a state of extreme discontent.

Left, two views of Mexico City

Above, suburban scene

Facing, one of the squares of Mexico City

The Palace of the Fine Arts.

The demonstration went ahead as planned, and both organizers and political observers were convinced that the government would clamp down harshly—though no-one dreamed that a full-scale massacre was about to take place. The total number of those killed may never be known; the government mentioned a figure of 15, but eye-witnesses have emphatically stated that some 400 persons died in the square itself and in the adjacent apartment blocks, and hundreds of others were wounded. In any case, this was an unspeakable massacre for which there is no valid explanation. Several days later, in an atmosphere of universal brotherhood, the principal countries of the world met in Mexico City, on schedule, to compete for the highest prizes of international sport.

However, the apparent totalitarianism of the régime should not mislead the reader, as the reality of Mexico is varied and surprising, with an ample dose of oriental philosophy. Besides deplorable events such as the massacre of Tlatelolco, Mexico has to its credit a number of political and social achievements which make it stand out among the countries of Latin America by virtue of its stability and progress, and, above all, its future prospects. Mexico will be the first of the countries of Latin America to break out of underdevelopment; this will be achieved, largely, thanks to the Mexican people them-

selves, who have a clear awareness of their past and present, their culture, and, in particular, of the mixed nature of their origins. In fact, their mixed blood, which they have succeeded in handling in an intelligent, no-nonsense way, is a source of pride and creative confidence for Mexicans.

Just as the Plaza de las Tres Culturas symbolizes the birth of a new people of mixed blood, the modern Plaza de la Constitución, more popularly known as El Zócalo, points to the origins of Mexico, and lies at the center of what was once a great empire and is now the vibrant metropolis of modern Mexico.

A map of the city drawn in about 1524 and attributed to Cortés, indicates a total surface of seven hundred acres, for a population of some 30,000.

Since that time, this city has swollen to a gigantic five million.

On September 15 each year, a festival takes place in the magnificent architectural setting of the Zócalo: it is the *noche del grito* ("night of the

Emperor Moctezuma and Mexico city before the Spanish conquest: this fresco, one of Diego Rivera's major works is in the National Palace.

shout"), in commemoration of the day in 1810 when a curate by the name of Miguel Hidalgo, in the small town of Dolores, in the province of Guanajuato, proclaimed Mexico's independence from Spain. On that historic night, Hidalgo rang the bell of his church in order to summon the people to rebel. The bell has since been take to the capital, where it occupies a place of honor at the center of the façade of the Palacio Municipal, the building which occupies the entire east side of the Zócalo. Nowadays it is rung by the President of Mexico, in the presence of the assembled multitudes, as a tribute to the heroes of Mexico's struggle for independence. After this symbolic moment, while the President joins with ambassadors, high government officials and public officials at an official reception in honor of the *noche del grito*, the crowds down in the Zócalo celebrate in their own way, with fireworks, confetti, music and folkdancing. These are the authentically Mexican festivities, put on by a people which still carries in its veins the blood of the ancient Aztecs who once founded a great culture on that very spot.

On the site of today's Palacio Municipal there used to be a huge structure known as the "old houses of Moctezuma". In pre-Hispanic times it

Emperor Moctezuma and Mexico City before the Spanish conquest: this important fresco by diego Rivera adorns the National Palace.

14

used to be the palace of Axayacatl ("water-face"), who reigned from 1469–81. This was where Cortés stayed on his first visit to Tenochtitlan, in 1519. This spot was the scene of two important events in the history of the conquest of Mexico: the assassination of Moctezuma, and the rout of the Spanish forces along Tlacopan Road on 30 June 1520—an episode famous in history under the name "noche triste".

Moctezuma was the king and priest who was ruler of Mexico when the Spaniards arrived. His reign lasted from 1502–1520. Like all his ancestors he was a superstitious man who unswervingly believed that the gods announced both good and evil to men, and that, apart from this divine message, there was nothing certain at all.

Accordingly, when the old king of Texcoco, Netzahualpilli, went to him and described visions in which he had seen all the Aztec cities in ruins, Moctezúma was horrified, since he felt that the old king's words were the gods' expression of an inexorable and highly unpleasant fate. The king of Texcoco also intimated that the Aztec army would suffer several defeats before the final collapse.

Shortly after the old king's visit, a priest wandering through the countryside at night saw a comet flash brilliantly across the black sky. When informed of this event, the king of Texcoco interpreted it as unmistakable proof of his

previous assertions about the fate of the Aztec empire.

The chroniclers tell us that Moctezuma, dismayed at this course of events, exclaimed: "If only I could turn into a stone, a stick or something, I would not have to endure the calamities that are to come. But what else can I do now, besides wait for these predictions to come true?"

Now thoroughly upset by these disturbing prospects, Moctezuma assembled all his chiefs and asked them if they had had any dreams recently. Since they failed to shed any light on the royal predicament, he consulted the elders, secretly hoping to obtain good news, about their past dreams. Three of them, however, described dreams which left Moctezuma even more distressed than before: the temples would be burnt to the ground, the fortifications would collapse and the Royal Palace would be flooded. On hearing this, the king became totally demoralized; feeling cheated, he had the three old men locked up and starved to death. Yet this decision, far from calming his mind, made him even more fearful.

It was the year Ca Acatl, *Reed One*; Moctezuma, overwhelmed by adverse omens, began to wonder whether an ancient prophecy might not be about to come true. 520 years before—or ten eras, in the Aztec calendar—when he left the city of Tula for the last time, Quetzalcoatl had

vowed that he would return to rule over the kingdom of the Toltecs, which, in Moctezuma's day was the territory under Aztec control.

Quetzalcoatl was a divinity who took the form of a plumed serpent; his many titles included those of god of the wind, of life, of monsters, and creator of men. He was also remembered as a highly civilizing influence.

According to the legend, the white and bearded Quetzalcoatl was a being who positively radiated a sense of brotherhood. He willingly shared his vast store of knowledge with the natives, and instilled in them a love for various arts and crafts. He gave them the basic skills essential for agriculture, and, in particular, the growing of corn. He also taught them to work with stone and precious metals.

Salvador Toscano summarizes the two major features of Quelzalcoatl the creator of men and giver of food, as expressed in indigenous mythology: "Quetzalcoatl actually created men: having stolen the bones of his ancestors and sprinkled them with his own blood in order to give birth to mankind, he then disguised himself as an ant, and stole a grain of corn form the Hill of Abundance—*Tonacatapetl*—to feed the men he had created." The strange legend which grew up around this fascinating person, who must doubtless have had some basis in historical reality, provides us with a source for the most varied conjectures. He was born in the year

Reed One, 947, and, according to the *Annals of Cuauhtitlan*, an indigenous manuscript of inestimable worth, he soon acquired the rank of priest, of king of Tula, and came to wield great power over his followers.

Chroniclers of the latter half of the 16th century, such as Ixtlixochitl and Duran, writing on the basis of the indigenous traditions, spoke of him as a bearded priest with a white skin, who had gone down in history as an incarnation of wisdom and chastity. As a priest, his activities were limited to fasting and mortification of the flesh in honor of the gods of the firmament. He never allowed human sacrifice, because he was so fond of his vassals, the Toltecs. Instead, his sacrifices were only of vipers, birds and butterflies."

Such an attitude provoked the wrath of the bloodthirsty gods, his enemies, who proceeded to wage a relentless war against him. They conspired and plotted in order to trap him. They made him look at himself in a mirror of obsidian, with its magic reflection and split image, in which a horrified Quetzalcoatl watched as time marched pitilessly across his face, marking it with age and decay. On another occasion, while Quetzalcoatl was fasting and abstaining in the temple at Tula, he was tempted by a deity wearing a serpent's mask made of mosaics and precious stones, and fantastically ornate feathers. The king was unable to resist the lure of this evil

17

being, and ran from the temple to find it. Lastly, the evil gods arranged for one of their number, Tezcatlipoca, to get Quetzalcoatl drunk with an alcoholic drink, *pulque*, which was fermented from the heart of the *maguey* plant. The king and priest lost the battle, and, under the influence of alcohol, committed incest and tarnished the purity of his life of penance and chastity.

Next morning, Quetzalcoatl was consumed by boundless remorse and anguish; he felt no longer worthy to be the leader of his people. After a long inner struggle with his conscience, he decided to leave Tula and, with it, his power and

glory. He fled, followed by many of his disciples, who were stricken with grief over the downfall of their priest-king. They crossed mountains and valleys until they reached the eastern sea, at a place named *Tilan Tlapallan Tlatlayan* ("the red, black burning place").

A huge bonfire was built near the sea for the martyrdom of the sinful king. He addressed his people for the last time, and announced that he would return to reign over them once more in the year Ca Acatl, *(Reed One)*, which, in the Aztec calendar, would coincide with 1519 in the Julian calendar—the year Cortés landed in Mexico. He then flung himself onto the blazing pyre. When he had been totally consumed by the flames, his heart rose up, in deified form, and turned into Venus, the dawn star which rises in the east *(Tlahuizcalpantecuhtli)*.

We can well imagine the thoughts that must have rushed into Moctezuma's mind one spring day in 1519, when a messenger from the Gulf coast rushed into his palace with sensational news: two floating houses had run aground off the coast, and strangely dressed men were landing from them. Juste skins and long beards.

It is highly interesting to note that Moctezuma sent Cortés, then at Veracruz, on the Atlantic coast, his royal regalia, which endowed him with all the splendor of Quetzalcoatl: the head-dress of long quetzal feathers depicting a royal eagle swooping earthwards, and the turquoise

mask adorned with two intertwined serpents.

Cortés sent all these marvels off to the emperor, Charles V.

However, let us go back for a moment to the Zócalo. The Palacio Nacional contains frescoes by the Mexican painter Diego Rivera, one of the country's great mural artists. The Mexican revolution of 1910–20 put an end to the bourgeois conformity of the colonial culture, and opened up new possibilities for artistic expression. The young intellectuals, painters and writers became the chroniclers of this movement of renewal.

Left: a characteristic Indian type. Above: one of the frescoes from the House of the Fine Arts, Mexico City (depicting the Spanish conquest).

19

The most impressive monument of the Zócalo is certainly the metropolitan cathedral. The main body of the church is independent of a Baroque structure which rests against it on its east side — the Sagrario Metropolitano. The striking difference between the cathedral and its annex derives from a difference in age. In the early 16th century, when the main church was being built, the services of the Sagrario were also held there; and it was not until 1749, at the height of the Baroque, that it was decided to build a separate Sagrario. The work was done by Lorenzo Rodriguez, who finished it in 1760. The construction of the cathedral took decades; although it was officially consecrated twice, in 1656 and also in 1672, by the viceroy of Mancera, the only part which had been concluded by the latter date was that situated directly under the middle of the main façade. By the end of the 17th century a start had been made on the east tower, and the main portico and west tower were both completed. In 1787, the city authorities, having decided that the towers should be finished, held a competition which was won by a Creole architect, José Damián Ortiz de Castro. While respecting the style of the completed sections he devised some truly ingenious solutions for the subsequent stages of construction. After his untimely death a new architect, Manuel Tolsan, was appointed.

The cathedral of Mexico City has always been

a center for devotion and, at the same time, a popular meeting-place. On any major religious feastday, the forecourt is crowded with people selling the most delightful handicrafts: straw figures of Christ, papier mâché dolls, spinning tops in seven colors, all kinds of whistles, pagan masks, and china, cardboard or tin figures of the Virgin Mary. Next to this fascinating and vivid display of folk art are the stalls selling food: corn-on-the-cob prepared in a variety of ways, corn pancakes, or *tacos*, which can be filled with anything you like, traditional native sweets, small doves made of corn. All this, and people, lots of people moving in and out of the church, through the forecourt, in a never-ending stream. At nightfall everyone goes home carrying something which they have found to their liking in this truly rewarding place.

Besides being the place where the people of Mexico City most love to go for a stroll, Chapultepec ("hill of the crickets") Park has uniquely close links with the main events of Mexican history. When the tribes which founded Mexico first arrived there, Chapultepec was a low hillock in the south-eastern part of Lake Anahuac. It was inhabited first by the Tol-

tecs and, from 1299 onwards, by the Aztecs. After the city of Tenochtitlan had been founded in 1325, King Izcoatl, ten years later, made it into a recreation area and a site for memorials to the Aztec kings, who were in the habit of having their likenesses carved into the rocks of this hill. Traces of these sculptures can still be seen today.

The poet-king Nezahualcoyotl built a palace at the foot of the hill and did the engineering work required to convey fresh water from the springs located there to Mexico City. It is thought that he also planted the *ahuehuetes*, the conifers which are still standing today. At the top of the hill there was also a structure which was used as an observatory, astronomy being one of the sciences which were highly developed by the Aztecs.

A decree of the king of Spain, dated July 25 1530, awarded the park to Hernán Cortés, the Conquistador, but he donated it to the city authorities for use as a place of recreation. Its new function did not diminish its importance as a supplier of water to Mexico City. There was a large reservoir from which the water flowed along aqueducts which followed the Tacuba and Veronica Roads, and the course of the present Avenida de Chapultepec, where some of its supporting arches can still be seen.

On high ground in Chapultepec Cortés had built a gunpowder factory which eventually

blew up, destroying the adjacent hermitage of St. Francis Xavier. This accident took place in 1784, and next year the viceroy, Matías de Gálvez, and his son Bernardo built a country residence—the Castle—on the ruins of ancient Aztec buildings.

In much more recent times, after the independence of Mexico, President Guadalupe Victoria tried to establish a botanical garden there, but the project ran into difficulties and ceased to exist after 1910. The establishment of the Military College in the Castle, in 1826, was to lead to the heroic defense, by the cadets being trained there, against the 1847 invasion by US forces. This episode is known as the *Niños Heroes*, or "child heroes".

Opposite left, picturesque display in the famous Lagunilla market.
Above, Chapultepec Castle. Facing, monument to India verde.

23

The Museum of Anthropology, which was opened in 1964, is situated to the north of the Paseo de la Reforma, in Chapultepec Park. This architectural ensemble, which is in many ways unparallelled in the whole world, was designed by the best Mexican architects and was based on the most modern nations of museum layout. It is a truly wonderful place to visit.

When the Spaniards reached Mexico they ruthlessly set about destroying the material remains of the defeated cultures. Their lust for gold was such that they melted down superb items of indigenous jewelry, while the "need" to supplant the native religions by the Christians faith led them to smash to pieces the magnificent statues of the local gods and demolish some extremely impressive temples. After their work of destruction was complete the Spanish conquerors often moved on, leaving the ruins behind them, but in most cases they built new, European-style towns on the same site. The entire monumental record of a people was thus buried beneath these new buildings, and beneath a thick layer of stupidity and ignorance. Only modern architecture has been able to make a serious attempt to read this historic message, which was so casually committed to oblivion.

In 1790, when digging was taking place on the Plaza Mayor in Mexico City, three formidable monoliths—now in the museum—were unearthed: the Stone of the Sun, the monument to Coatlicua and the monument to the victories of Tizoc. Fortunately for Mexican archeology, a distinguished Mexican who was deeply devoted to his nation's past took an interest in these re-

mains and wrote a book on two of the stone monuments which had been recovered. He was Antonio de León y Gama. Thanks to his efforts, and against the whole previous trend with respect to indigenous ruins, the monoliths were preserved, the Stone of the Sun near a wall of the cathedral, the monuments to Coatlicua and Tizoc in the University. Such, in fact, was the origin of the Museum of Anthropology. In 1825 official protection was extended to the recovery of legal monuments, and vast numbers of objects began to accumulate in a large hall at the University. Though the items thus assembled were not in any particularly scientific order, these early efforts resulted in the recovery and saving of many unique objects. The increasingly admirable display which was being accumulated in this hall attracted the attention of Maximilian, who decided to create a national museum and set aside for this purpose the old palace on Calle de la Moneda, in Mexico City.

This museum was a hodge-podge of pre-His-

panic objects, items recalling the history of modern Mexico and natural history collections. It was not until 1940 that a rigorous selection was made, and it was decided to devote the museum exclusively to anthropological collections. At the same time, there was mounting interest throughout the country in the recovery of as much as possible of the ancient cultural heritage of Mexico: excavations proceeded apace, with the firm backing of governments. As new marvels poured in from all corners of Mexico, it soon became evident that the museum's current premises were much too small.

It then occurred to those concerned that it would be better to build a new museum, more worthy of the memory of the indigenous cultures, and a permanent school by virtue of the layout of its rooms. The museum was, after all, to be a historical museum, and not an art museum. In the words of Ignacio Bernal "the fact that many of the objects are genuine works of ancient art is a fine addition to the principal message: to help Mexicans know and understand, to the extent possible, the meaning of the indigenous Mexico, and to relate it to the Mexico which is being built today".

The museum occupies an area of 125,000 square yards, 45,000 of which are under cover, while the open areas, such as the central courtyard and the entrance plaza, add another 36,000. It contains twelve halls.

The visitor first enters a room which is a sort of introduction to Mexican anthropology. This is followed by a description of the various cultures of the peoples of Central America, discoveries pertaining to the earliest human presence on the American landmass (25,000 BC) and the pre-classical cultures of the plateaux. Rooms 5 and 6 are devoted, respectively, to Teotihuacan and the Toltecs, and room 7, the largest of all, deals with the Mexicas or Aztecs. The Mayas occupy room 10. The other rooms illustrate the civilisations of the other regions of the country, in particular the Zapotecs, the Mixtecs, Olmecs, Totonacs and others, from the north and west of Mexico.

It is no exaggeration to say that the Museum of Anthropology, on its own, is sufficient to justify a visit to Mexico City. It is a truly unforgettable experience. The wealth of objects it contains is a most fitting response to the arrogance of the men who, having come to this country from a more highly advanced civilisation, took it for granted that the culture of the "savage" peoples was only worthy of contempt.

After its foundation in 1551 the Royal and Pontifical University of Mexico grew in a somewhat loose manner for many years, taking over several historic buildings which, though officially designated as premises meant to accommodate various faculties and institutes of higher learning, were really ill-suited to this

Various views of the University of Mexico: the Palacio de la Administracion, the park, the campus, the library and a fresco on an outer wall.

purpose. For these reasons, in 1953, a large area to the south of the city was chosen for the construction of a modern university city, grouping together the faculties and schools which had previously been scattered all over the city. The chosen site is covered in petrified volcanic lava which was formed thousands of years ago by an eruption of the volcano Xitla which buried a primitive culture of the middle pre-classical period (1,100 years BC). A pyramid belonging to this culture was saved and placed on the university campus.

The architect of the University City was Carlos Lazo. The total surface area occupied by the city is 1,800 acres, 923 of which are urbanized. It has 16 miles of paved roads, 39 bridges, 105 acres of green space, and four million ornamental trees. It also contains a stadium with seating capacity for 90,000. Several of the façades of the university buildings are decorated with frescoes by the best known Mexican mural painters. All of the facilities and structures are modern, and were designed for a long life, despite the steady increase in the number of Mexicans seeking admission. The sheer size of this University City can also be conveyed by the fact that its library has a capacity for more than two million volumes; it also has a large medical center and a botanical garden.

As an artistic entity the University City of Mexico is a *must* for any visitor to Mexico City.

27

The visitor to Mexico City tends to take his bearings from the Paseo de la Reforma, a long avenue bordered by big hotels, airline offices, travel agencies, luxury shops, banks, etc. It was inaugurated in 1865 by Maximilian, and, until 1867, was known as the Paseo del Emperador, in his honor. Its present name was given it by President Sebastián Lerdo de Tejada, who also widened it and enhanced it by the addition of numerous trees.

From about 1882 onwards the Mexican bourgeoisie began to build their mansions along the Paseo, and 1889 saw the opening of the Café Colón, which was for many years the most chic and sophisticated coffee house in the entire capital. About this time monuments started to appear on the *glorietas*, or traffic circles along the Paseo, among them the monument to Christopher Columbus, done in the Italian Renaissance style by the French sculptor Charles Cordier, and that dedicated to Cuauhtemoc, which is the work of a Mexican sculptor, Miguel Norena. Near the Cuauhtemoc glorieta there is a small square with a monument to Pasteur, a gift to the city from the French community.

But the most popular of all the monuments along Reforma is the one to independence, referred to locally as "the Angel". This is a column, with neo-classical influences, ending in a gilded angel. This work, by the architect Antonio Rivas Mercado, was inaugurated in 1910. On the section of the Paseo that runs from the downtown area to Chapultepec Park stands the statue to Diana the goddess of hunting, by the sculptor Juan Olaguibel. Simón Bolívar, on horseback, gazes down the avenue from another *glorieta*; this work, by Manuel Centurion in 1944, was a gift to the people of Mexico from Venezuela. Lastly we come to the monument built to commemorate the courage shown by Lázaro Cárdenas, a Mexican president who returned to his country all the oil-wells which were in the hands of United States companies. This monument was also by Juan Olaguibel.

Mexico is rich in convents from the colonial period, almost all of which are of great historical interest. One of the most superb of these is the Convento de la Enseñanza, which was founded by a rich heiress, María Ignacia de Azlor, the Countess of Santa Olaya. It was virtually completed in the remarkable period of six months, in 1754. Writing of the Convento de la Encarnación, the historian Mariano de las Cuevas had the following to say: "The cloisters built by the nuns of the Incarnation was a most stately structure; in more modern times it has been restored, or maybe one should say, profaned by the kind of monstrous paintings that issue forth from certain types of brain, under the influence

Left, the famous monument known as "El Angel", erected in honor of the independence of Mexico. Facing, scene from a bull-fight. Below: a view of the famous Paseo de la Reforma.

of the worst sort of marihuana. It was built late in the 17th century through the generosity of an exceedingly rich and Christian gentleman by the name of Alonso de Lorenzana." The smoker of marihuana alluded to by the Reverend Cuevas was none other than Diego Rivera, who painted some frescoes in the interior of the convent—which at the time was being used as the offices of the Ministry of Education, on the instructions of José de Vasconcelos, one of Mexico's great thinkers, statesmen and writers, who was then Minister of State. This commission occurred towards the beginning of Rivera's long and prodigious career as a muralist.

Other buildings similar to the convents mentioned above, are the colleges of San Ildefonso and Las Vizcainas.

The promenade and park of La Alameda are one of the most pleasant places in the whole of the city. The Spanish chronicler Salvador Novo, who knew Mexico very well, describes La Alameda as follows: "If we walk along the entire length of La Alameda, 555 yards, and across its breadth of 280 yards, observing the layout of the place carefully as we go, we will notice that its surface area is divided into four quarters, at the

29

Facing, the landscape of the highland plateaus, northwest of the capital. Below, rural scene in the same region.

intersection of the major and minor axes of the central figure. Each of these four quarters also has the shape of a parallelogram subdivided by its respective diagonals. Through these and other subdivisions, the entire surface area forms 24 triangles and 7 circles with ornamental fountains."

From Mexico City, situated at 6,900 feet above sea level, highways spread out in all directions across this vast country, half as large as Europe, which contains every imaginable type of landscape, from virgin forest to snow-capped peaks, including the gentle Mediterranean climate of certain coastal regions.

Two thirds of Mexico are occupied by a huge plateau, which, framed by the eastern and western Sierra Madre ranges, stretches all the way from the United States border to the great vol-

canic barrier which straddles Mexico from Veracruz, on the Atlantic, to the city of Colima, on the Pacific.

The plateau is divided by the imaginary line of the Tropic of Cancer into two large independent zones: the arid or semi-arid northern deserts, and the Central Plateau.

The Central Plateau is both the geographic heart and the vital center of Mexico. This is where the major cities are located, together with most of the country's industry and commerce.

The average altitude of the Central Plateau is slightly over 6,000 feet. The climate is moderate; the rainy season, which lasts from May to October, sometimes involves flooding which makes some roads impassable.

The steepest and most beautiful valleys in Mexico are situated near the line of volcanoes,

the peaks of which exceed 12,000 feet. These areas contain huge coniferous forests, with delightfully pure air: for example, the superb valley of Toluca, at 8,000 feet, which, apart from its striking natural beauty, also has some important ruins. Numerous mountain streams flow down from the snow-capped peaks, some of them eventually forming large rivers, such as the Balsas and the Grande de Santiago.

The cities are located in the river basins and on the plains. The soil is fertile, and, besides the yew-leaved fir, there are large forests of mixed species (oak, pine walnut,) and grasslands which provide excellent grazing for cattle. Agriculture is well developed, and produces a great variety of fruit and vegetables, in addition to *frijoles* (black beans), corn and other cereals.

Not far from major mining and industrial centers such as San Luis Potosí and León are smaller cities which still have a distinctly colonial flavor, for example Guanajuato, the home of Diego Rivera, the town in the state of Dolores where Hidalgo so loudly proclaimed the independence of his country, and also Querétaro, where Maximilian was shot. The central plateau

Left, the countryside around Querétaro. Facing at Toluca, the Palace of the Governor of the State of Mexico. Below, Indian types.

has an abundance of mineral wealth; indeed Mexico is, with Canada, with largest producer of silver in the world. The plateau also produces large quantities of precious stones, including opal, amethyst, agate and rock crystal.

The population is for the most part of mixed race. The Whites, according to one estimate, account for only 5% of the total, whereas the aboriginals who still preserve their ancient customs live only in the most inaccessible mountainous regions.

Most of the inhabitants of the rural areas live in houses of brick or adobe, with sloping roofs. The ubiquitous *sarape*, worn by the peasants, is a brightly colored cloak with an opening in the middle for the head. Because of rapid changes in temperature, the country folk use it as a type of overcoat, tied at the waist with a string for ease of movement in the fields. Country women go about in a *rebozo*, which is a kind of wrap, used not only to keep warm but also as a protection against unwelcome male attention, and as a way of transporting young children.

The diversity of landscapes and the mixture of races and cultures have combined to produce an extrovert, baroque Mexican type, both passionate and enigmatic, with characteristics which may at first sight seem contradictory. All the more reason, then, to visit and seek to understand the different civilisations which flour-

Below, Indian women talking. Facing View of the picturesque village of San Miguel de Allende and its impressive church. Opposite facing, the Baroque church of Tepozothan. Lower right, old houses at Guanajuato.

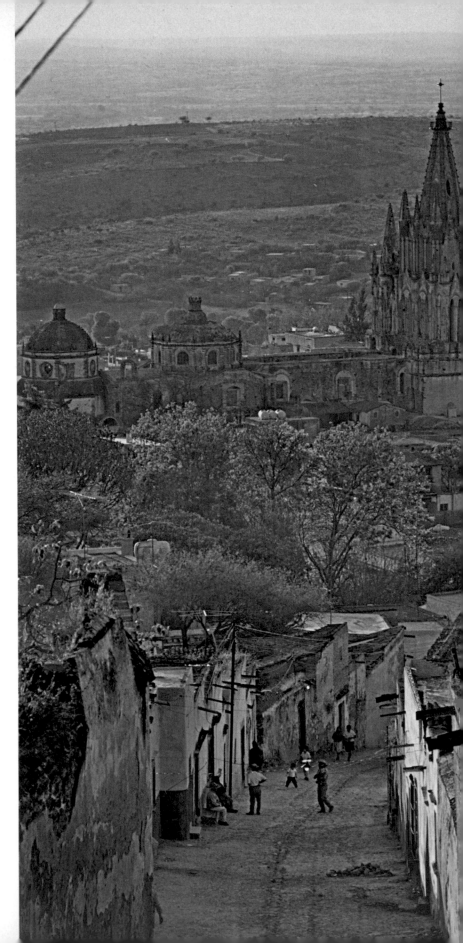

ished at one time or another in this country, in order to decipher the character of the Mexican people of today.

Teotihuacan, 30 miles north east of Mexico City, was the site of the civilisation of the Toltecs (first 800 years of the Christian era), who can really be regarded as the ancestors of modern Mexico.

The built their capital city (meaning "place of god") on the ruins of an earlier settlement.

The culture of Teotihuacan was based on religion, to such an extent that it can truly be called "the city of the gods". Perfection was to be achieved through the logic of geometry. The simplicity and flawless beauty of its numerous temples and public buildings are harmoniously integrated into a great central axis known as the "Avenue of the Dead" (Calzada de los Muertos).

This avenue crosses the city for over a mile, with a gradient of some 100 feet. At its highest point it opens onto the Pyramid of the Moon, from which the visitor has a sweeping view of the most grandiose urban complex of the pre-Hispanic world.

Half-way down the broad Avenue of the Dead, so named because the Toltecs originally

The Toltec remains of Teotihuacan, with the famous Pyramid of the Sun.

Supporting pillars of a house at Teotihuacan. Right, the "modern" buildings of Tula.

thought that the knolls surrounding it were tombs, the 200-foot Pyramid of the Sun towers above the entire landscape.

At the south end of the avenue the Toltecs built their most perfect architectural structure, the one which is the sublimation of their whole spiritual world: the Citadel.

A series of broad platforms were built to form a vast square, 400 yards long, enclosing a large inner courtyard, access to which was provided by a staircase leading down from the main street. There, in the middle, stands the Pyramid of Tlaloc (god of rain) and Quetzalcoatl.

The presence of so many rectangles and horizontal surfaces gives the citadel an almost supernatural appearance, in sharp contrast with the undulating mountains all around. The prodigious artistry of the Toltecs is most apparent on the *tableros*, or facing of each of the superimposed segments of the pyramid, on which the heads of the gods alternate: the plumed head of the serpent jutting forward aggressively, with fierce eyes made of obsidian, and an undulating, stylized body, the mouth wide open as if to shout, and, next to it, the stark contrast of the highly abstract and unreal mask of the god of rain, made of circles and prisms.

The rectangle, which was the ultimate artistic shape in the culture of Teotihuacan, also appears in their sculpture, most particularly in the "goddess of the living water" (Chalchiuhtlicue):

38

this geometric figure occurs in all details of this work, from the single block of stone used for the sculpture down to fine detail such as the goddess's toes and the beads on her necklace.

The decline of the Toltec city began in the 18th century, and was perhaps symbolized by the use of moulds for the manufacture of ceramics. The entire city and its glorious past were destroyed by a huge fire.

The last of the inhabitants of Teotihuacan moved away from the ruins of their city and founded new settlements in neighboring regions. Tula, 20 miles to the north, was one such city.

The god Quetzalcoatl, in the person of one of the priests of Teotihuacan, came to Tula in the 9th century and proceeded to carry out certain religious and social reforms, including, as we have seen, the abolition of human sacrifice.

Unlike Teotihuacan, Tula was not an exclusively spiritual city. Instead, it was dominated by the warriors whose effigies can be seen in every one of the monuments in the city. The geometrical style still prevails, but the mask, being a divine trait, has disappeared.

The pyramid of Tlahuzcalpantecuhtli stands on one side of the great ceremonial square: it consists of five structures, with splendid bas-reliefs of warriors, tigers and various other animals. All that remains of the temple which originally towered over the entire pyramid is the four colossal figures of stone, which used to support its roof.

These, the most important sculptures in Tula, were made from four perfectly matching blocks of stone over fifteen feet high.

The remains of the Palacio Quemado ("Burnt Palace") are situated next to the pyramid, amongst a number of other buildings. Its columns, though incomplete, are still standing. It was here, during excavations, that the enigmatic sculpture known as the *Chac-mool* was discovered.

The face of the Chac-mool is so human that it could hardly be meant to represent a god. It is lying on its back, with both head and knees raised, and with a tray, intended for offerings, resting on its belly. In all probability this is the figure of a warrior, since, like them, it is wearing sandals, it bears the solar butterfly on its shoulder and is carrying a knife in its left hand. This altar-like figure occurs in various places in Mexico, and at different periods.

The warriors of Tula always feared the arrival of an enemy from the north. They therefore sought to protect the temple from the antici-

The Toltec remains at Tula. The temple of the Morning Star. The photograph shown at the top of the right-hand page is that of a recent discovery.

The splendors of the Mexican Baroque, at the convent of Tepozotlan (16th century) a vault, the façade of the monastery, an altar.

42

pated invasion by building in front of it a wall adorned with a large and very beautiful bas-relief covered with serpents devouring skulls; the top of the wall is in the form of elegant and rather curious battlements patterned on the shape of a snail.

If these brave warriors were to die in battle they enjoyed the honor of accompanying the sun on its daily journey when they reached the next world. Being sun-worshippers they erected a pyramid in honor of the sun, to whom they dedicated their strange game of *pelota*, which was also found in many pre-Cortesian civilisations.

On an H-shaped track, the players worshipped the almighty sun, in a ceremony which combined elements of both religion and sport, by trying to get a rubber ball through a stone ring *(Tlachtemalacatl)* secured to the wall of the central passage.

The dreaded enemy from the north, in the form of the Chichimecs, appeared in Tula in 1168, overrunning and burning the city, despite the brave resistance of its warriors. The survivors moved away to the south, as far as Yucatán, where they mixed with the Mayas.

The Chichimecs were aggressive nomads, cavemen who used to wear the skins of the animals they hunted. Having originally lived in various parts of the valley of Mexico, they became more sedentary after the destruction of Tula, making their capital in Tenayuca. In the center of the city they built a large pyramid to which they added a new structure once every 52 years.

The sole god of the Chichimecs, the one for whom they lived and died, was the Sun.

The visitor is confronted with the rather chilling sight of hundreds of statues of aggressive serpents surrounding the entire pyramid and jutting out over its various embankments. These fearsome cratures, which the Chichimecs painted in various colors, depending on the direction in which they were facing, were supposed to maintain a watch over the sun's trajectory.

The Chichimecs can be considered as the closest ancestors of the Aztecs.

The Federal Democratic Republic of Mexico consists of 29 States and two Territories, the latter being the most sparsely populated areas, at opposite ends of the country: one of them in the Californian peninsula, and the other, Quintana Róo, in Yucatán.

Facing "shops" at Tula. Below, view of El Caracol (*salt evaporation plant, near Lake Texcoco*).

The States of Sinaloa, Nayarit, Jalisco, Michoacán and Colima, all of which are situated on the Pacific Coast, form what is known as the Western Region; this region was the site of ancient cultures whose common denominator was pottery.

Ceramics is one of the handicrafts which was taken root most deeply in the Mexican people, so much so that no peasant house is without earthenware pots of some sort or another. In any case, according to the popular wisdom of the country, food always tastes better if it has been prepared in a earthenware pot. Using the techniques which the Spanish colonists brought with them, such as the potter's wheel and kiln-glazing, Mexicans have refined their pottery and ceramics, using a great variety of shapes and colors.

The ancient cultures of the western part of Mexico attached no importance at all to architecture, for the simple reason that, as far as they were concerned, the religious question did not exist. Their cities lacked gods, and, consequently, temples. They only built tombs, and in so doing displayed an advanced funeral art. Their small sculptures were intended to perpetuate life—a notion which lingers on, in latent form, in the Mexico of today.

Clay was the perfect medium for the worship of the dead. In Chupicuaro, one of the centers of this form of art, the clay figurines of divinities

were always based on the human body.

The clay sculptures found in Colima and Nayarit, however, are much more lifelike.

In Colima, for example, the dominant style is naturalism in motion: warriors, players, dancers, laborers, persons from everyday life are all depicted in such a way that their inner emotions are brought to the surface; their features tell a tale of love, eroticism, tenderness, sensuality, strength, humor . . . This vitality is true also of the superbly portrayed animals, particularly the well-fed dogs which are shown in the most varied positions—sleeping, growling, eating, panting, and, surprisingly, laughing and crying.

In the region of Nayarit there was less diversity of shapes and expressions. Here, instead, of the naturalistic classicism of Colima, we have a type of expressionism, in which aesthetic considerations are discarded for the sake of emphasis, often accompanied by extreme exaggeration. The results include an open, unashamed kind of sexuality, physical deformities, huge nostrils, and stunted or over-long legs or arms.

The clay cultures of the western Mexican civilisations, though heavily influenced by the idea of death and burial, were nonetheless full of joy and life.

Above, the valley of Toluca.

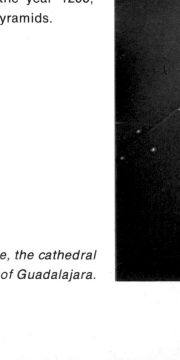

The capital of the State of Jalisco, Guadalajara, is situated on the banks of the Río Grande de Santiago (altitude 5,000 ft.), near the Pacific coast, in the midst of a rich and fertile plain. It has a population of over one and a half million.

Guadalajara is a major industrial and commercial center, which, on account of its climate and the nature of its people, is one of the nicest places in Mexico. Its inhabitants, largely descended from the relatively jovial ancestors of the western regions, have made theirs a bright, gay city, whose broad avenues are adorned with flowers, and whose women, in the words of a popular song, are renowned for their beauty. Parts of Guadalajara have preserved the colonial style, which is still to be seen in the splendid cathedral, with its heterogeneous influences, and a large number of Baroque churches, while the contemporary and even futuristic architecture of certain other parts of the city are wholly of the 20th century.

In common with Mexicans as a whole. the people here are highly religious, the main object of their piety being the popular Virgin of Zapopan. Her image is borne aloft in processions on certain dates through the different districts, in the hope that her intercession may be invoked against flooding. In each parish the protective Virgin is received with much pomp and fervor.

The visitor will be amply rewarded not only by the city, but also by the surrounding countryside which is in many ways ideal for vacations. 25 miles south, along the shores of Lake Chapala, many residents of Guadalajara have built summer homes. And they could hardly have chosen a better place, as both the climate and the landscape are extremely restful. On the Pacific coast, at Puerto Vallarta, tourists who like sun, sand and bright lights will find a resort which is at least the equal of Acapulco.

Half-way between Guadalajara and Mexico City, whether by road or plane, the traveller can make a brief detour to the beautiful Lake Pázcuaro and visit the island of Janitzio, which is inhabited by indigenous people whose livelihood is based on fishing . . . and also tourism. Or he might wish to go to Tzintzuntzan, capital of the Tarascans, built about the year 1200, which has left us five original pyramids.

Above, the cathedral
of Guadalajara.

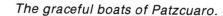
The graceful boats of Patzcuaro.

The valley of Puebla is one of the highest in the country, together with the valleys of Mexico and Toluca. The 85 miles between Mexico City are an easy and pleasant drive along a good divided highway, in the midst of impressive mountain scenery. The gigantic uniform mass of the volcano Popcatepetl looms ahead throughout this entire trip; indeed its snowy peak almost stands astride one's path, like a forbidding colossus. One skirts the foothills of the volcano on the way into Puebla.

Puebla is an industrial and mining town. It was here, in the Fort of San Javier, that the Mexicans defeated the French—a victory which has been made into a national festival.

Spanish influence is very noticeable in the special kind of decorative tile for which Puebla is renowned throughout Mexico. Other handicrafts include pots, plates, cups and other domestic utensils, made in a wide variety of patterns and in the most vivid colors.

The local women often wear an embroidered blouse and a skirt of various colors, which, according to legend, was designed by a Chinese slave from Puebla, and is thus known as *china poblana*. This same name is used of the local country women.

Between the eastern Sierra Madre and the Gulf several regional cultures flourished after the fire which destroyed Teotihuacan.

In Cholula, near Puebla, there is a gigantic

A procession in the country near Querétaro. Right, the astonishing remains of Mexcaltitlan (Guadalajara).

Left, landscape in the Puebla region; middle, view of the town of Puebla and its typical 18th-century houses. Facing and below, two views of the famous Popocatepetl (16700 ft.).

The ruins of El Tajin, a Tatonec city.

pyramid dedicated to the god of the rain; this structure is unique in the whole of Mexico, in that it is covered from top to bottom with steps. As we move north towards the sea we enter the tropical region of Tatonacapan, with the rather solemn city of El Tajín, which is well worth a visit.

In the pre-Cortesian period the inhabitants of this area made small clay figurines depicting scenes from daily life and also phallic symbols. For reasons of prudery, or the greed of collectors, or both, most of these latter have been removed to the secluded basements of museums or been added to already large private collections.

When confronted with gods of the classical period, the artists of El Tajín limited their range of topics, choosing henceforth to concentrate on warriors and dancers. They produced hundreds of such figures, most of whom, curiously enough, are laughing.

The Tatonecs, who founded the city, were obliged to clear the dense tropical forest in order to make way for their architecture; yet it was not long before the jungle-like vegetation moved in again, after the city had been abandoned and deserted, and completely covered up most of their monuments. It was not until 1785 that one of the gems of Mexican architecture, the Pyramid of the Niches, was discovered. This structure consisted of seven super-imposed masses, each surrounded by an elegant cornice. The broad facing of each of these levels is pitted with 365 niches, one for each day of the year, on all sides of the pyramid.

This pyramid is truly a monument to rhythm and harmony. Its horizontal aspect is nicely offset by the rigid staircase, whereas the brilliant light is broken by the shadows cast by each of the niches.

When the last inhabitants of El Tajín moved out, they went south and settled in Cempoala. This city was the first major populated area found by the Spaniards as they landed on the Gulf coast. The first Mexicans of mixed blood were produced by the inter-marriage of the Conquistadores with the local inhabitants of this area.

Christianity spread to Mexico soon after the arrival of the first Spanish forces. The three religious orders entrusted with this task were the Augustines, Franciscans and Dominicans.

The ancient Mexican gods and their images apparently disappeared, and were replaced by vast numbers of Catholic churches. In the first century of Spanish occupation alone about three hundred were built, not counting the numerous stone crosses and chapels which sprouted up everywhere, on roads, squares and

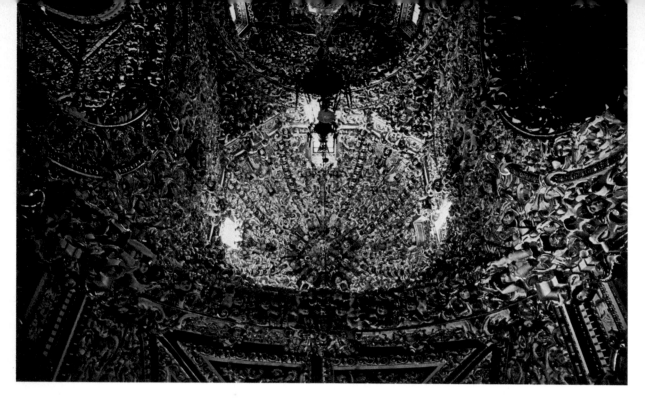

The instructions of Spanish architects were carried out by Indians who often managed to work into their structures certain details reminiscent of their ancient idols, such as crosses with obsidian mirrors, tufts of feathers, etc. Even today, in a small country church, one is quite likely to see, side by side, the gods of rain and sun and the Virgin, together with others figures of Catholic saints.

Religious temples which display a clear Hispanic influence can be found anywhere in the republic, but they are particularly frequent in the valley of Puebla.

The cathedral is a fine example: it is a gaunt structure made of grey stone, with the outline of the doorways in white and the cupolas covered with tiles.

The Church of Our Lady of Tonantzintla, a few miles from the city, is perhaps the most astonishing sample of this kind of religious art in the

Puebla area. It is the pinnacle of Mexican Baroque: a world of dazzling colors and shapes, in which the Mexican of mixed blood has poured out his imagination, giving the whole work a truly fantastic air. Ever since the church was first built, it was the parishioners themselves who, over the years, have gradually changed and accumulated the ornamental detail, in keeping with their own inspiration, wishes and tastes. At various times an assortment of angels, scrolls, arabesques and spiralling columns were added, together with a whole welter of ornamental detail which surrounds the statue of the Virgin and converges on the point, high on the cupola, where the Holy Ghost seems to be the focal point of this flamboyant display of folk art. For the Mexican people religion is a matter of passion, almost of metaphysical violence. Religious occasions provide an opportunity for ceremonies in which the five senses predominate, and in which spirituality is only skin-deep.

Left, a vault of the church of Santa Maria of Tonantzintla, at Cholula. Facing, handicrafts.

ALFARERIA DE CURIOSIDADES

On a hill, on the outskirts of the capital, there was once a temple to the goddess Tonantzin, mother of Quetzalcoatl. It was here in 1530, that the Virgin Mary is said to have appeared, with the features of an Indian woman, to a simple shepherd named Juan Diego. Astonished by this vision, he asked for some evidence which he could show to the world, to bear witness of this great moment. In response, the Virgin threw a bunch of roses onto the Indian's cape. Juan Diego then went before the bishop of Zumarraga, but, when he turned the fold of his cape, he found, instead of a bunch of roses, the image of the virgin of Guadalupe, imprinted for ever on the cloth. The news spread quickly throughout the country, and thousands of Indians became converted to Catholicism. Ever since then, the image of the Virgin of Guadalupe has become the most celebrated religious image in Mexico.

On all subsequent anniversaries of that event, on 12 December, the apparition has been commemorated. Pilgrims come from all over the country to prostrate themselves at the feet of the Virgin with the Indian features; many of them cover the last 2½ miles of the pilgrimage on their knees, in order to give thanks for some favor which had been granted to them, or as an act of penance. The outpouring of popular sentiment is not, however, entirely penitential, as it is accompanied by much singing and dancing in the nearby square.

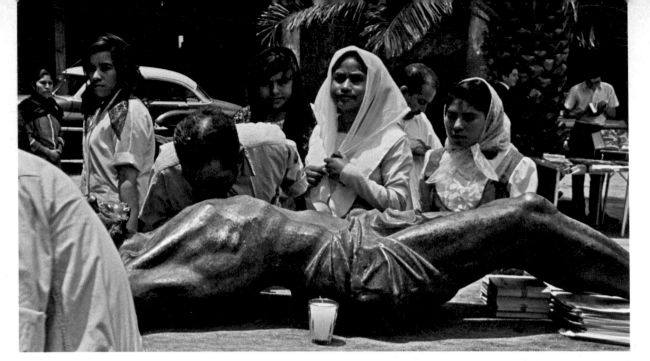

*Left, half-caste kissing a statue of Christ crucified. Below,
scene from Good Friday procession. Above, undertaker's.*

Successive earthquakes, and the passage of time, caused the walls to crack in several places, with the result that the Mexicans built a new and much more modern, functional church next to the ancient Basilica, which could no longer safely accomodate so many pilgrims. The new structure was inaugurated in 1976.

The Día de los Muertos is another major event in the Mexican religious calendar. In common with many of his ancestors, the Mexican of today continues to honor the dead. On the night of 1 November the cemeteries are filled with candles, votive lamps, flowers and foodstuffs which are offered to the dead relatives of the faithful. The ubiquitous emblem of this occasion is the skull *(calavera)*, which is made of different materials. About this time large numbers of similar items are on sale: candy in the shape of bones, plastic skeletions, ornate skulls made of clay ... The children go around carrying pumpkins with holes for features, and a lighted candle inside.

The image of death is a familiar component of Mexican folk art, though it is not always taken seriously. Skulls occur time and time again in drawings, paintings and bas-reliefs, both artistic and popular.

In Mexican literature, for example in the famous novel *Pedro Paramo*, by Juan Rulfo, the characters often communicate with their dead. In fact, departed ancestors act as if they were still alive—and not as ghosts, but as ordinary persons of flesh and blood.

In one of the paintings of Diego Rivera, entitled *Sueño de una tarde dominical en la Alameda Central* (Dream on a Sunday afternoon in Central Park), Death, elegantly clad, is holding a child by the hand, and takes the arm of what one assumes to be the head of the family, surrounded by its other members. The overall effect is a family snapshot posed before a fairground photographer.

59

One should really travel around the whole of Mexico in order to form a full understanding of the country. However, the short trip from Mexico City to Acapulco neatly sums up the mixture of cultures, the changes of landscape and, in general, the contrasts which are to be found in this great nation.

As the traveller covers the 200 miles between the capital and this coastal resort he is constantly taken from the past into the present. The change in altitude alone is staggering— from nearly 7,000 feet to sea level.

After leaving the city on the Autopista del Sur the traveller first comes across the floating gardens, which are a sort of natural park forming an enclave among the remains of the former lakes of this region. On public holidays the people come here with their lunch baskets to have a good time. 50 miles out of Mexico City, in Cuernavaca, one is already down to an altitude of just over 3,000 feet, much to the relief of those whose are not accustomed to great altitudes.

The balmy climate and splendid colonial architecture of Cuernavaca have made it a favorite with tourists and Mexicans alike. The better-off residents of the capital often buy second homes here. The city has much to offer, particularly the beautiful Borda gardens, the cathedral, the Palace of Hernán Cortés with the splendid frescoes by Rivera, and a beautiful Baroque convent.

60

Left, two typical Mexican courtyards, gaily bedecked with flowers. Right, various views of the picturesque town of Taxco (founded in 1529).

A mere 12 miles further on, and one has slipped back into history, in the ancient city of Xochicalco. This city, which, being built on the top of a hill, offers a fine view of two valleys, was constructed on different levels, according to the slope of the land. The whole city is crowned by a great pyramid covered with superb bas-reliefs. Only a short distance away is the *pelota* court where it is claimed that this ancient sport was invented, and from which it spread to other parts of Mexico. The name of the city means "in the house of the flowers". Much of Xochicalco remains buried, awaiting the full revelation of its many secrets.

A short distance to the south one emerges from the ancient world and enters the present day again, in the picturesque town of Taxco. The fine Baroque church is well worth a visit.

Little remains of its former splendor, however, except a kind of tranquil nostalgia among its people. Now down to 16,000 inhabitants. Taxco is struggling to survive, and, in so doing it has gone in for tourism, with particular stress on high-quality gold and silver jewelry.

Across the basin of the River Mezcala the road passes through the site of another ancient culture, the legacy of which consists of figurines which are extremely soft to the touch, and which are colored green, grey or black. Centuries before the modern Cubists, these ancient sculptors suggested the human figure on the basis of

flat surfaces which they cut in the stone.

The final straight, as it were, takes us into Acapulco, where we plunge totally into the bustling modern age.

For many foreigners, Acapulco is synonymous with Mexico. This famous resort, nestling below the hills and framed by the magnificent bay, stares at one from the glossy brochures of travel agencies the world over.

With its boulevards, its cosmopolitan beach, its palm trees, its tropical atmosphere, its luxury hotels, and its various attractions such as the spectacular *clavado de la muerte,* Acapulco is a paradise for certain types of tourist.

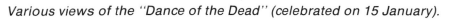
Various views of the "Dance of the Dead" (celebrated on 15 January).

The remains of Monte-Alban.

From the volcanic belt, the Sierra Madre del Sur stretches all the way down the Pacific Coast. The valley of Oaxaca is situated in the southern part of the range.

The city of Oaxaca, the capital of the State of the same name, became the preferred residence of the Spanish *conquistadores*, so that the indigenous people had to flee to the surrounding mountains.

The area was originally inhabited by two hostile peoples, the Zapotecs and the mixtecs. It was not until the Aztecs invaded their territory that their respective kings united their armies for their common defence.

The Zapotecs were the first to have a period of greatness. These highly religious people were convinced that they had descended from wild animals; in fact, as part of their worship of those animals they built the architectural complex at Monte Albán.

"The inhabitants of the land of the clouds", which is the etymology of the indigenous word *Mixtec*, were men of heightened artistic sensitivity who were responsible for the most perfect works of the pre-Hispanic world and whose influence extended as far a most of the other civilisations of Meso-America. Their artists were in great demand at the courts of various monarchs other than their own.

In Mitla, to the west of Monte Albán, the Mixtecs created a City of Palaces. These buildings are simple rectangular galleries, with flat ceilings, arranged in such a way that they were always separated from one another by a completely closed courtyard.

The striking thing about theses palaces is that all the walls are covered with magnificent mosaics and huge horizontal Grecian-style frets. The inhabitants of Mitla were uniquely skilled in mural decoration, both interior and exterior. Even their tombs are decorated with fine relief cut straight into the rock.

The consummate mastery of the Mixtecs was most evident, however, in the their work with metals and semi-precious stones. The three hundred objects recently found in a tomb at Monte Albán illustrate the extreme sophistication of their art: finely carved marble vessels, goblets of rock crystal, knives, necklaces, earrings, polychromatic ceramics and forty assorted items made of gold, each of immense value.

The Spanish *conquistadores* themselves, according to their chronicles, were deeply impressed by the items of gold and silver which

they found, though this did not prevent them from melting huge piles of these priceless objects into ingots, for shipment back to Europe.

The Mixtecs used two main techniques: *repoussé* work on fine sheets of gold, on which they impressed patterns and relief, and an original process known as the "molten wax" process. The latter technique took the following form: first, they modelled the figure with a soft mixture of carbon and clay; then they covered it with a layer of beeswax, to which they added a clay shape with a hole at the top and another at the bottom. Through the upper opening they poured the molten gold, which dissolved the wax and took its place, causing it to flow out the bottom. Then, all that remained was to break open the mould.

Besides the ruins of Monte Albán and Mitla, the city of Oaxaca, at the end of the valley, is itself well worth a visit. Since this city was the last point held by the Spaniards, its numerous monuments in the colonial style are in an excellent state of preservation.

Oaxaca was the birthplace of Benito Juárez, one of the great figures of Mexican history. This Indian, of Zapotec ancestry, studied law and eventually became the governor of the State of Oaxaca. He was sent into exile on account of his liberal ideas, though he later returned to his country to lead his people in the struggle against the French and Emperor Maximilian.

70

Facing and above, views of a Christian church at Mitla, built on the ruins of a pre-Columbian temple, with some of its masonry. Right, wooded slopes in the Chiapas region.

His birthday, 21 March, is celebrated as a national holiday, with the title *Día del niño indio* ("Day of the Indian child").

The distance between the Gulf of Mexico and the Pacific Ocean across the Isthmus of Tehuantepec is only 120 miles. As one crosses it, one leaves behind the regions of valleys and towering peaks, and enters dense tropical forest, and the world of the Mayas.

The States of Tabasco and Chispas lie in the wettest areas in the world. The soil is astonishingly fertile—so much so that one can actually *see* certain plants and shrubs growing. These dangerous forests stretch all the way to the border of Guatemala, in the south. One of the species of tree which grow in them is the *zapote*, from which *chicle* is extracted. At one time many deaths occurred among those who ventured into the forests looking for this valuable product, and who were bitten by reptiles and insects.

Yet it was precisely among such inhospitable

Two characteristic landscapes in the Chiapas region.

vegetation that the Mayas chose to settle, cutting away vast clearings in the forest, around the year 1,500 BC. The Mayas, who were of Asian origin, as their features testify, began to grow corn on the cleared land, gradually increasing the size of the cob by judicious cross-breeding with other varieties. In this way they succeeded in boosting the size and form that of the original cob, which was both irregular and tiny, to one the size of a thumb, and later, by repeating the process, to the size we know today.

Then as now, corn and *frijoles* were the basic food of the people; the Mayas supplemented it with pumpkin, cocoa and tapioca. They sometimes used cocoa beans as currency.

With the passage of time the Mayas invented the calendar and hieroglyphic script. The elements, such as rain, thunder, light and dark-ness, acquired a magic significance; indeed, the Mayas thought that they could control them by means of special rites and ceremonies. This in turn led them to the discovery of religion, and, with it, the need to build temples and cities—which they then proceeded to do, reaching a pinnacle of beauty and splendor which has truly earned them the title of "the Greeks of the New World".

The Mayas occupied the whole of southern Mexico and much of Guatemala and British Honduras. Sylvanus G. Morley, a great expert in their culture, classified as many as 120 archeological sites, and calculated a Maya population of between 13 and 50 million, varying according to the period and the circumstances. This gives one an idea of the proportions of the Mayan civilisation.

The remains of Pa-
lenque, the most im-
portant center of the
Maya civilization.

The Mayas were great masters of astronomy, architecture and sculpture, and had a brilliant social and political life. The main difference between their culture and these of other peoples of Meso-America is the absence, in what remains of the Mayan civilisation, of tragedy and cruelty. Their religion was pervaded by tranquillity, beauty and sensuality. Even feelings associated with the moment of death were expressed by the Mayas in a calm and humane way.

In one of the open spaces which the Mayas had cut out for themselves stand the remains of the city of Palenque, one of the centers of the first Maya civilisation. The forest looms close to the site, and the brilliant sun combines with the extreme damp of the marshlands to make the visitor feel that the sea is only a few miles away. One is quite literally enveloped in damp heat, light and an overpowering shade of green.

A stream, which the Mayas had partly channeled along an aqueduct, divides the city in two. The Palace is doubtless one of the major pieces of Maya architecture: its tower, which consists of three segments, is unique in the pre-Cortesian world.

The walls are covered with reliefs. The Mayas used stucco, a soft material composed of slaked lime and sand which, with time, becomes as hard as stone, in order to give eternal form to their artistic yearnings. The sculptures at Pa-

lenque are the finest of their entire history.

However, we still have what we may regard as exceptional evidence of the Maya genius. This is the first, and so far the only, crypt inside a pyramid. It was first discovered in 1949. The entrance is in the Temple of the Inscriptions. The explorer Alberto Ruiz happened to lift a flagstone, and discovered a cleverly concealed staircase leading down some 130 feet to a new triangular passageway, guarded by six skeletons, which in turn led to a large chamber. In the middle of this chamber he found a stone, under which lay a sarcophagus containing the remains of a priest wearing a jade mask and surrounded by all manner of jewels and offerings.

The city of Bonampak was built on a hill in the Chiapas range, in the midst of a virgin forest near the Guatemala border. The area is now inhabited by the Lacandon Indians, who cling insistently to their traditions and are quite out of touch with our modern civilisation.

The traveller who ventures that far will be rewarded by the spectacle of the Temple of the Paintings, and in particular its walls. In 1946 the explorer and photographer Giles J. Healey persuaded the tribes living in the area, the descendants of the Mayas, to let him see these

magnificent frescoes.

The building consists of three enclosures with sloping roofs. The walls are completely covered with paintings which enable us, better than bas reliefs, to form a precise idea of the customs, rites, dress and weapons of the Mayas. These frescoes show us in detail the preparations for a ceremony, followed by a battle and eventual victory; we see the victors standing proudly by, silhouetted against the sky, while the defeated enemy flees in disarray. The series of pictures ends with a great feast, complete with spectacular dances and offerings to the gods. The human figure dominates throughout these paintings. Men from a wide range of social positions are depicted in numerous different postures, with little variation in pictorial treatment or in emphasis on light and shade: their bodies are a sepia color on a brilliant orange or blue background, depending on whether they are shown indoors or out-of-doors, respectively.

Above, small, simple country altar, in the region of Chichen Itza. Right, bamboo plantation, at Uxmal. Below, dwellings in an Indian village in Yucatan.

The Yucatan Peninsula lies on the Gulf of Mexico and the Caribbean. The landscape is in the nature of a steppe, with a tropical climate and a very low rainfall which is due to the warm sea winds.

Mérida is the main city in Yucatán. As the visitor strolls through its markets and plazas he will notice that the whole place has a very relaxed air about it. The descendants of the Mayas still have many of their features, besides an innate elegance in the gestures and movements. The men wear the traditional white *guayabera*, a kind of shirt which is typical of the whole Gulf area, while their womenfolk wear the extremely

attractive *huipil*, a white cotton tunic which reaches down to the knees. This beautifully embroidered garment is worn with an open neck, often over a lace petticoat.

The *maguey* or *pita*, which in Yucatan is known by the generic name *nenequen*, is the most important commodity of the region. This plant, which has broad fleshy leaves rimmed with spines, and yellow flowers, occurs all over the peninsula, in more than 200 species. Through incisions in the trunk, the maguey secretes a sweet liquid which is used to make liquor—*soltol* in northern Mexico, *tequila* and *pulque*, the latter being the most popular drink

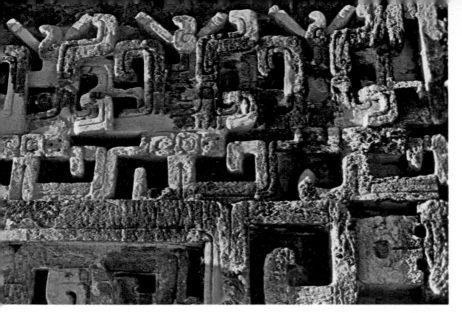

of the ordinary country people. The fiber of this plant, *sisal*, which is both pliable and tough, is used in the manufacture of rope, cord and all sorts of wickerwork.

The markets of Yucatán are a colorful sight, and contain a wide range of tropical products and local handicrafts.

The *machete* is the favorite tool of the inhabitants of this part of Mexico. They use this weapon, above all, when clearing a path through dense forest, or cutting the maguey, sisal or sugar cane.

The *jacal*, which closely resembles the huts depicted in the Mayan basreliefs, is the main type of dwelling of the rural population. This wooden or bamboo structure has a single rectangular room, with two doors, one opposite the other, for ventilation. One thing common to all homes in Yucatán is the hooks, secured to the walls, from which hammocks are hung at night. The people of Yucatán sleep in hammocks and usually advise visitors to do likewise.

Nowadays more than 80,000 people speak nothing but Maya, which, together with Nahuatl, Otomi, Mixtec and Zapotec, is one of the major aboriginal languages.

The Maya remains of Chichen Itza: the temple of the Thousand Columns, and detail from a mural sculpture.

Right, various views of the monuments of Uxmal and an expressive sculpture at Chichen Itza.

Chichen-Itza, Uxmal, Kabah, Sayil and Tulum are the principal archeological sites in Yucatán, though there are many more besides. All of the ancient Maxa cities are accessible by road from Mérida. This is an area of savannahs, which is sharply different from the region around Palenque, on account of its low rainfall. Man's response to this lack of water has influenced all his activities.

Living in a region without any significant rivers, the Mayas sought to remedy their perennial thirst by leaning heavily on their gods, who were the only supernatural beings capable of helping them. Their worship of Chac, the god of rain, took some rather extreme forms.

Chac pervades the whole of Maya architecture, like an oft-repeated refrain or incantation.

Though dry on the surface, Yucatan has large numbers of underground streams some of which have caused the ground to subside, thus forming the famous *cenotes*, or natural wells. The Mayas built their cities close to these magic holes in the ground which they regarded as a gift from the gods. The Sacred Cenote became a center for religious ceremonies, and the culminating point of solemn processions; richly adorned young men and women were thrown down between these smooth, dark walls as an offering to the gods. The monumental scale of Chichen-Itza strongly suggests that it must have been the capital of its age, a place of pilgrimage to which people came from the remotest parts of Meso-America.

Another of the mythical gods of Mexico, Quetzalcoatl, also perpetuated his presence at Chichen-Itza, having been brought there by the Toltec migrants from Tula.

In Maya Quetzalcoatl came to be known as Kululan, and it is under this name that the most important pyramid of the center of Chichen-Itza was dedicated to him. This is a monument in which everything has its significance: the four staircases have a total of 365 steps; each of the façades has 52 *tableros* (this being the number of years in the Toltec century); the segments of the pyramid, as divided by the steep embankments, contain 18 parts, equal to the number of months in the Maya calendar, and the stairs themselves face each of the four points of the compass. Nowhere, in the whole of pre-Hispanic Mexico, is there another building in which the symbols have been so subtlely integrated into the whole structure or in which symettry has been taken to such heights of perfection.

The pyramids, the sacred *cenotes,* the *pelota* courts, the Temple of the Warriors, and the group of the Thousand Columns, the quadrangle of the nuns, the *Chac-mooles,* etc., all of which combine to give Chichen-Itza a well-merited place in the history of the great cultures of the world.

Left-hand page and below, Maya ruins in the immense forest of Yucatan. Facing, two descendents of the Mayas and, above, specimens of tropical birds from the forest.

The cathedral and the Palace of Merida.

Swimming pool of an hotel at Uxmal and the tropical vegetation in the garden of another hotel, at Chichen Itza.

On account of the horse-shoe shape of the Gulf of Mexico and its proximity to the warm waters of the Caribbean the whole of the coastal fringe has a typically tropical climate. The remains of ancient cultures, often surrounded by giant vegetation, are in sharp contrast with the modern industrial and agricultural scene around cities such as Tampico and Veracruz.

Veracruz is now the most important port of Mexico, as it was in the time of the Spanish occupation and the brief imperial period under Maximilian.

The coast of the State of Veracruz is a perfect illustration of the range of colors, smells and tastes associated with the tropical climate. Like the Cubans and other inhabitants of the West Indies, the people of this part of Mexico have some Negro blood in their veins; their faces are on the whole rounder than elsewhere in Mexico, and they are, by temperament, gay and jovial.

The coconut tree, which can grow to a height of some 100 feet, and the palm-tree grow near the beaches and in sandy soil generally; further inland are the caobo and the cedar, both of which produce very good quality timber. The whole region is rich in natural beauty, particularly birds, plants and flowers.

The fruit of this region is what the traveller from less exotic parts usually finds most impressive. The tropical markets of the Gulf coast contain a tempting array of the most delicious

fruits, all of which, even if they are available overseas, have a unique and unforgettable taste when bought and eaten in the area where they are grown.

It was in this tropical region of Mexico, in the 8th century BC, that the Olmec civilisation came into being. At La Venta, Tres Zapotes and Cerro de las Mesas some important Olmec architecture, with the recurrent theme of the jaguar occurring throughout, can still be seen today.

The jaguar, the largest of the New World tigers, has a yellowish coat with black spots, and lives in the forests of Mexico. This ferocious animal, which has been given divine form in all the civilisations which occurred at various times in the territory of Mexico, shows its face, in either natural or abstract form, in many of the principal monuments.

According to legend the jaguar mated with a woman, and they brought forth a race of titans: the Olmecs. Only thirty years have elapsed since the discovery, in the forests of Tabasco and Veracruz, of a number of monumental heads made of single blocks of stone about 15 feet high. These are thought to be images of priests, the intermediaries between men and gods.

One is truly flabbergasted at the sheer size of these sculptures, which have a child's face and a tiger's mouth. No two are alike. Their deep stare expresses great spiritual power, and their thick fleshy lips are unmistakably sad.

Despite its extreme age, the Olmec culture has only just been discovered, and it is quite possible that many of its artefacts and monuments may still be buried or lost in the forest.

Besides huge plantations of cocoa, coffee, tobacco and sugar cane, the Gulf of Mexico contains another sort of wealth, with a distinctly modern image—oil.

Exploratory drilling was first done in 1901, whereas there are now some 3,000 wells. The average annual output is 135 million barrels, placing Mexico eighth in order of magnitude among the world's oil producers.

The largest refineries are in Tampico and Veracruz. Since 1938, the date of the expropriation of oil resources, all the oil produced in Mexico has been controlled and distributed by the State.

Top, the tropical coast of Cozumel and remains from the period of the conquest, on the Caribbean coast, near Tulum. Left, detail from a sculpture, at Chichen Itza. Facing, an astonishing Olmec head, at Tabasco (Yucatan).

89

*Giant cactus
from the State of Guerrero.*

The north of Mexico is also a land of myth. In many legends and folk tales it is thought of as an El Dorado, a fascinating land which lures men on in the quest for adventure and gold and then leads them to their deaths. The names of many places in this region have become famous in the countless films which Hollywood, for better or for worse, has devoted to Mexican adventures over the years.

Northern Mexico is also the home of two famous leaders from the time of the Revolution: Alvaro Obregón and Pancho Villa. Together with the leader of the southern peasants, Emiliano Zapata, they promoted the uprising of the Mexican people.

By means of intrigue, Porfirio Díaz succeeded Juárez in 1876. For 35 years he then clung to power, inflicting on the country a sad period in its history—one in which the workers and peasants suffered the most cruel exploitation, which was imposed on them in the name of law and order.

Farm workers were virtually slaves, and often did not even manage to collect their pitiful wages. The government felt invulnerable. However, the discontent spread even to the liberal landowners, one of whom, Madero, was the first to call for an end to the dictatorship.

When the Spaniards first arrived in Mexico, in 1519, the country had about five million inhabitants. This figure dropped sharply during the first few years of the Spanish conquest, because of the fighting and also the diseases which the Europeans had brought with them, eventually reaching a low of about two million. Mexico now has 50 million inhabitants, more than half of whom live in rural areas.

Racially speaking the country is mainly of mixed blood *(mestizo)*. The poorer farmhands are called *Indians* in popular usage, this pejorative title contrasting unfavorably with the word *Mexicans* with which city-dwellers refer to themselves.

On the whole, the Indians, or the mass of the rural population, lead a pretty tough life. In order to survive, they often depend on an annual harvest which may not always be very abundant; they react stoically to calamitous weather, of whatever sort, and, in general, to the circumstances of under-development, though it must be noted that, among the countries of Latin America, Mexico is remarkably stable and well organised. Hoping to find a stable income, rural workers often migrate to the big cities, where they find themselves living, on arrival, in cramped, makeshift quarters out of town.

This constant uphill struggle has not, however, made the Mexican peasant a grim, downtrodden type. On the contrary, they display remarkable vitality, gaiety and ingenuity. The country people always seem ready to smile, and to follow a philosophy which consists essen-

Left, melons, mangoes and water-melons cut into slices, and chicharrones (pork fritters). Facing, view of a rodeo, and, below, the ceremony of the Charruada, in which 18th-century costumes are worn. Right, musicians and folk ballet.

ket, they travel on the picturesque and ramshackle buses which are so much a part of the Mexican rural scene, and which take little heed of offical timetables or fixed stops. Visitors find this mode of travel, and particularly the time it takes, quite astonishing. In a typical scene, a mother sits waiting by the side of the road, with a pile of bundles and assorted baskets, while her children are off playing in a nearby field. Eventually the bus lumbers into viev, spewing out a black and evil-smelling smoke, whereupon the entire family assembles, nervously and happily. But the bus is crammed full of people and objects and simply does not stop. As it disappears over the brow of the hill, the woman sits on her milestone again, with infinite resignation and patience, takes out her knitting and settles down for a long wait. The children return to their games. Yet they may have to wait another ten or twelve hours for another bus.

tially of a tough brand of home-made optimism.

When they need to go to the nearest town to go shopping or to sell their produce in the mar-

The market is a favorite meeting-place for Mexicans. And for anyone seeking to get to know Mexico, the market is a *must*: the motley arrays of goods on the different stalls, the clamor, laughter, the to-and-fro have something peculiarly Mexican. Prices are always the subject of intense haggling, since they are not fixed. Both men and women take part in this process

Left, Indian women. Below, a man plays the part of the village idiot. Right, stall in the region of Taxco.

with gusto; one might even say that the seller would regard as a slight if one were not to launch into the game of offer, counter-offer, etc.

Most of the markets are indoors, though the *tianguis*, or out-door markets, can still be found in rural areas. Tianguis is the name given to the canvas which is laid out on the ground to display merchandise, and it is also used of the canopies erected in the market-place against the sun.

The visitor will find everything in these markets: fruit, vegetables, meat, fish, baskets, pots, ornaments, religous images, etc. Folk art is very widespread in Mexico. Handicrafts serve the people in their everyday needs, provide a source of income from the tourists and also serve simply as a means of expression for the able and agile hands of the Mexican craftsman. This popular art takes many forms and uses many materials, from clay to gold and silver.

Every city in Mexico, besides its market-place and its church, has its own *Zócalo*. This term, which means pedestal, has an interesting history. It had been intended to build a monument to the independence of Mexico in the main square of Mexico City, though the project never got further than the construction of the pedestal. The name *zócalo*, however, stuck, and came to denote not just the huge open square in the capital, but all similar places in the cities of Mexico. This square is the scene of popular

94

meetings, popular festivities and the typical Mexican Sunday.

By virtue of their national temperament, and possibly also as a means of compensating for their daily grind, the Mexican people really let forth a torrent of energy, and also of lavish expenditures, on certain days of the year.

Popular music is a steady background noise which follows one everywhere during one's travels through this country, in streets, bars, homes, buses, squares. The popular dance known as the *jarabe*, and the popular songs which make up such an important part of the folk culture of Mexico, sum up the life of the country. In the *corridos* and *rancheras* we hear of the adventures of great folk heroes, the beauty and delights of their women, of love, passion, vengeance, the Revolution. Indeed, the whole of the history of Mexico is literally sung in this way.

The *Mariachis*, the famous street-musicians with their striking black costume and enormous sombreros, accompany the soloist on trumpets and violins, and also play at bull-fights.